Dunham+Company
6111 W. Plano Pkwy., Suite 2700
Plano, TX 75093
dunhamandcompany.com

Printed in the United States of America

MILLENNIAL DONORS
They're Not Who You Think They Are

CONTENTS

INTRODUCTION

The Millennial generation (those born between 1982 and 2000) has in many ways become the center of attention. And for good reason.

- In the U.S., according to U.S. census data from 2015[1], Millennials are now the largest generation, numbering over 83 million, compared to 75 million Baby Boomers.
- Research is showing that Millennials are more engaged in philanthropy than many thought. According to Blackbaud's 2013 NEXGEN report[2], 60 percent of Millennials gave to charity at that time, whereas 84 percent gave to charity in 2014, according to the 2015 Millennial Impact Report.[3]
- When looking at the makeup of charitable donations, Millennials give 11 percent of donations, compared to 20 percent from Gen Xers, 43 percent from Boomers and 26 percent from Matures.[4]

The upshot is that over the course of the last few years, fundraisers and charities have become more focused on the Millennial generation... wondering what makes Millennials tick... wanting to understand their preferences, interests and engagement with the charitable sector...

... and what the implications might be for charities as they seek to engage this generation.

So we set out to find out directly from Millennial donors what they support, the level of that support, what prompts them to give, general attributes and attitudes... and how they compare to other generations of donors. In addition, we didn't limit our study to the U.S., but also studied donors in the United Kingdom and Australia to better understand how Millennials in the U.S. compare to their counterparts in those countries.

In the following pages we unpack the findings and as you will see, Millennial donors really aren't who you think they might be.

RICK DUNHAM
CEO, Dunham+Company
MAY 23, 2017

[1] http://www.census.gov/newsroom/press-releases/2015/cb15-113.html
[2] The Next Generation of American Giving, page 6, published August 2013.
[3] http://www.themillennialimpact.com/research/
[4] The Next Generation of American Giving, page 6, published August 2013.

> *Millennials are no longer the next generation; they're the now generation. Those who want to thrive in the future must understand who this generation is today. This study by Dunham+Company is a clear picture of who Millennials really are and how to effectively engage them as donors.*
>
> **WES GAY**
>
> *FORBES UNDER 30 CONTRIBUTOR*

METHODOLOGY

For this study we tapped our research friends at Campbell Rinker who conducted a 15-minute online survey of 1,391 U.S. donors, 648 donors in Great Britain, and 619 Australian donors. Donors were screened to ensure they had given at least $20 to a charity in the past year.

The researchers used a stratified random sampling methodology to proportionally recruit donors from four different generational groups:

MILLENNIALS // (BORN BETWEEN 1982-2000)
GEN XERS // (BORN BETWEEN 1965-1981)
BOOMERS // (BORN BETWEEN 1946-1964)
MATURES // (BORN BEFORE 1945)

Millennial donors were oversampled to allow for more robust cross-cohort comparisons.

At the 95 percent confidence level, the study delivers a margin of error of ±2.6 percent in the U.S. and ~+3.9 percent in Great Britain and Australia. The results among Millennials provide a ±3.2 percent margin of error overall, ±4.3 percent in the U.S. and ~±6.6 percent in Great Britain and Australia.

After fielding, the researchers weighted the response by generations within each country to reflect the actual proportion of those generations in the national population. During fielding, the lack of available older respondents in Australia necessitated altering the sampling quotas for older donors.

A big thanks to the Editorial Review Team for their hard work and helpful insight:

GREG GORMAN
CEO
GREG GORMAN COMMUNICATIONS

TOM PERRAULT
Global Director Digital Services
DUNHAM+COMPANY

DIRK RINKER
President
CAMPBELL RINKER

MICHAEL LEWANDOWSKI
Senior Digital Strategist
DUNHAM+COMPANY

NICK PITTS
Director of Cultural Engagement
DENISON FORUM

JENNIFER SPENCER
VP of Custom Research
CAMPBELL RINKER

NOTE: All currency has been converted to U.S. Dollars, with the conversion rate for British Pound Sterling set at 1.25 and the conversion rate for Australian Dollars at 0.75.

GENERAL FINDINGS

Let's begin by setting the context for giving by Millennials by looking at how their annual giving compares by generation. As you might expect, U.S. Millennials do not give as much to non-church charities as other generations.

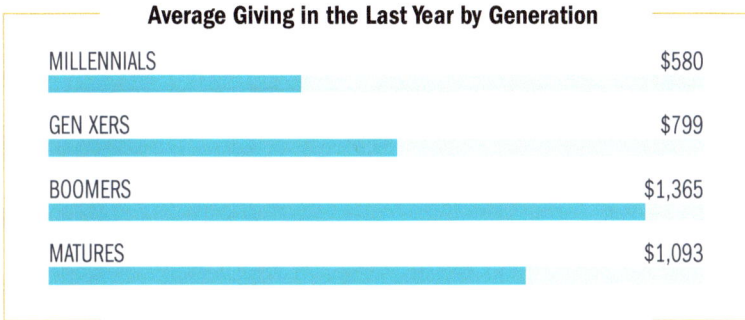

Average Giving in the Last Year by Generation

MILLENNIALS	$580
GEN XERS	$799
BOOMERS	$1,365
MATURES	$1,093

But in looking at Millennial giving in the U.K. and Australia, their level of giving is much more similar to the other generations.

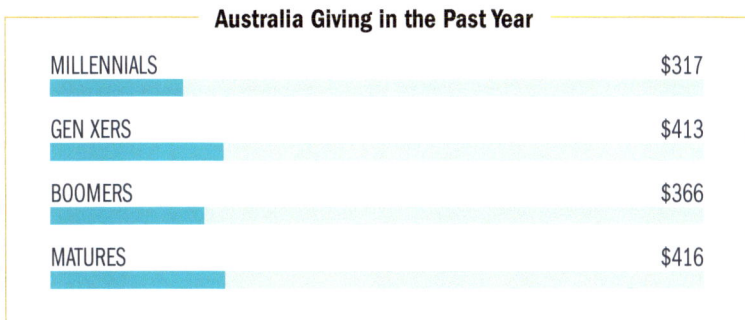

U.K. Giving in the Past Year

MILLENNIALS	$234
GEN XERS	$245
BOOMERS	$276
MATURES	$259

Australia Giving in the Past Year

MILLENNIALS	$317
GEN XERS	$413
BOOMERS	$366
MATURES	$416

MILLENNIAL DONORS
Who gives the most?
(In the past 12 months)

$580

U.S.

$234

U.K.

$317

AUS

In looking at how Millennials compare in giving to non-church charities by country, U.S. Millennials are significantly more generous than their U.K. and Australian counterparts, giving 147 percent more than U.K. Millennials and 83 percent more than Australian Millennials.

Many wonder how this compares with other generations when they were the same age as Millennials today. The one report we can point to for the U.S. is the *Women Give 2016* report.

In this report, researchers compared giving behavior across a 40-year period, consisting of the Mature Generation (those born before 1945) to Millennials when they were young adults, ages 25 to 47. "The study found that Gen X and millennial single women today give at about the same level as pre-boomer single women did in the 1970s. At the same time, Gen X and millennial single men and married couples are giving at lower levels than did their pre-boomer counterparts."[1]

[1] https://www.bbh.com/en-us/insights/shifting-patterns-in-charitable-giving-over-time/18970

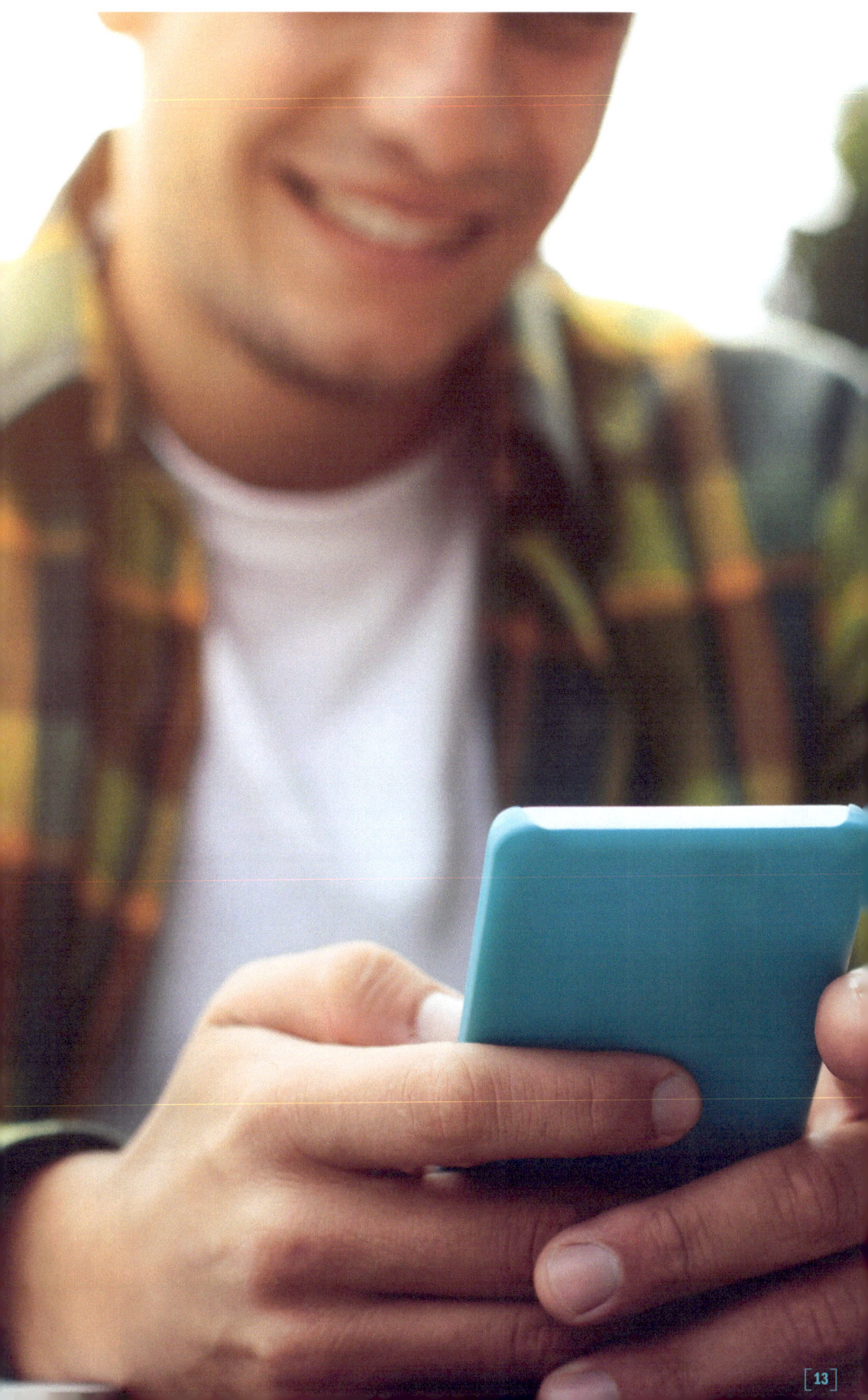

MILLENNIAL DONORS AND VOLUNTEERING

We also wondered about volunteering. Generally, U.S. donors (67 percent) are significantly more likely to volunteer compared to donors in the U.K. and Australia (~50 percent). The same holds true just for Millennials, with U.S. Millennials having volunteered 40 hours in the last year compared to 30 hours for U.K. Millennials and 28 hours for Australian Millennials.

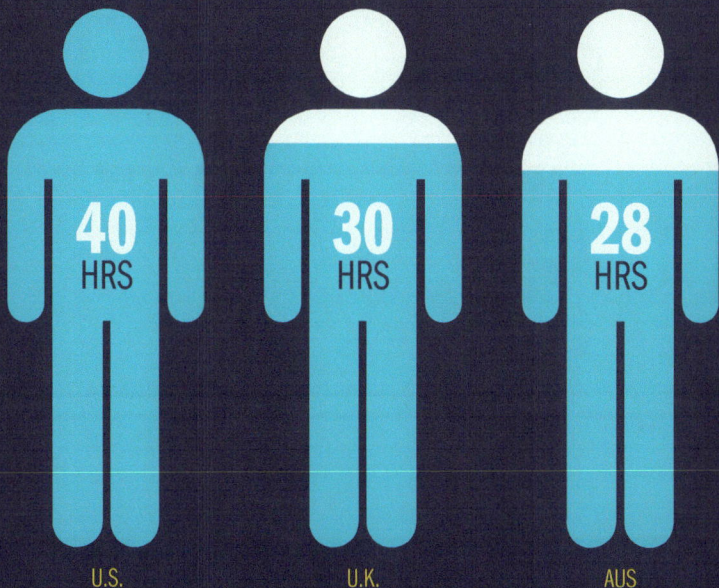

MILLENNIAL DONORS
Who volunteers the most?
(per year)

40 HRS

30 HRS

28 HRS

U.S.   U.K.   AUS

In looking at volunteering specifically in the U.S., over the last year Millennials volunteered less than Boomers and Matures and more than Gen Xers.

VOLUNTEERING
(In the Past 12 Months)

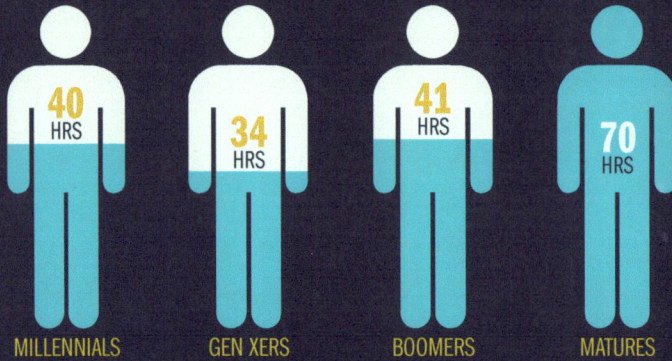

40 HRS — MILLENNIALS

34 HRS — GEN XERS

41 HRS — BOOMERS

70 HRS — MATURES

A study led by Jean Twenge out of San Diego State University substantiates this slight change. Focusing on the generational differences in young adults' life goals, concern for others and civic orientation, Twenge and company found:

Millennials and GenX'ers scored lower than Boomers on the majority of items measuring concern for others, though most of the differences were small. Compared to Boomers, Millennials were less likely to have donated to charities, less likely to want a job worthwhile to society or that would help others... They were less likely to want to work in a social service organization or become a social worker, and were less likely to express empathy for outgroups. In the sole significant exception to these trends, Millennials were more likely than Boomers or GenX to participate in community service during high school.[1]

[1] https://www.apa.org/pubs/journals/releases/psp-102-5-1045.pdf

WHERE MILLENNIALS GIVE

One of the things we wanted to find out was what kind of charities Millennials like to support. As you can see from the following chart, U.S. Millennial donors are more likely to support places of worship and faith-based nonprofits compared to other generations.

THE TOP THREE TYPES OF CHARITIES BY GENERATION:

MILLENNIALS

$416
PLACES OF WORSHIP

$96
FAITH-BASED NONPROFITS

$84
EDUCATION

GEN XERS

$868
PLACES OF WORSHIP

$126
EDUCATION

$113
HEALTH/MED

BOOMERS

$1,472
SOCIAL SERVICES

$1244
PLACES OF WORSHIP

$819
HEALTH/MED

MATURES

$1,369
PLACES OF WORSHIP

$260
EDUCATION

$146
ARTS & CULTURE

Millennials give more than five times the amount to places of worship and faith-based nonprofits than they do to education, their next highest area of support. This high level of support for places of worship is mirrored in the other U.S. generations and speaks to the important role faith plays in the life of U.S. donors regardless of their generation.

In looking at how U.S. Millennials compare to their counterparts in the U.K. and Australia, we found that they give much more to support places of worship. The chart below shows how their giving breaks out when considering the top three types of charities Millennials support in these countries.

THE TOP THREE TYPES OF CHARITIES MILLENNIALS SUPPORT ARE:

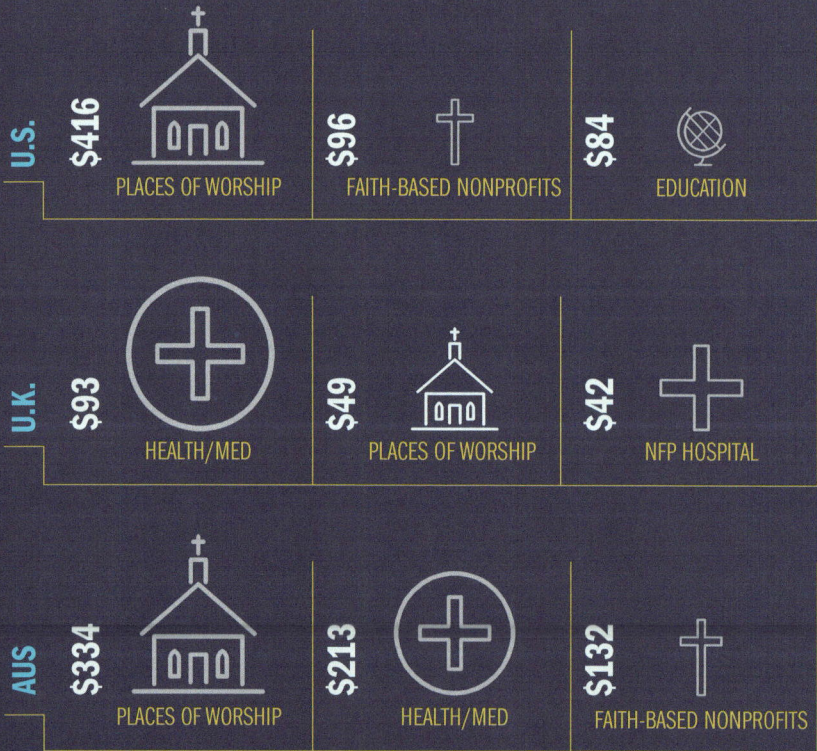

U.S.

$416 — PLACES OF WORSHIP

$96 — FAITH-BASED NONPROFITS

$84 — EDUCATION

U.K.

$93 — HEALTH/MED

$49 — PLACES OF WORSHIP

$42 — NFP HOSPITAL

AUS

$334 — PLACES OF WORSHIP

$213 — HEALTH/MED

$132 — FAITH-BASED NONPROFITS

What is important to note is the significant support for faith-related activity in the U.S. and Australia compared to the lesser import that has for U.K. Millennials. The proportion of Millennial support adds an important layer of context to these figures. While 71 percent of U.S. Millennials report giving to their place of worship, just 56 percent of Australian Millennials echo that behavior, along with 60 percent of British Millennials.

MILLENNIAL DONORS
Who gives to their place of worship?

U.S. **71**%　　U.K. **60**%　　AUS **56**%

RELIGIOUS INVOLVEMENT

Seeing the high level of support that Millennial donors have for places of worship and faith-based nonprofits, naturally we wanted to know how often they attended religious services.

As you can see from the accompanying chart, Millennial donors in the U.S. are about as likely to attend religious services at least weekly as Gen Xer and Boomer donors (25 percent, 27 percent and 28 percent, respectively), with Matures much more likely to do so at 36 percent.

Of interest is that U.S. donors are significantly more likely to attend religious services than their counterparts in our other countries. Unsurprisingly, there is less of a variance between Matures in the U.S., U.K. and Australia.

CHURCH ATTENDANCE
Once a Week or More

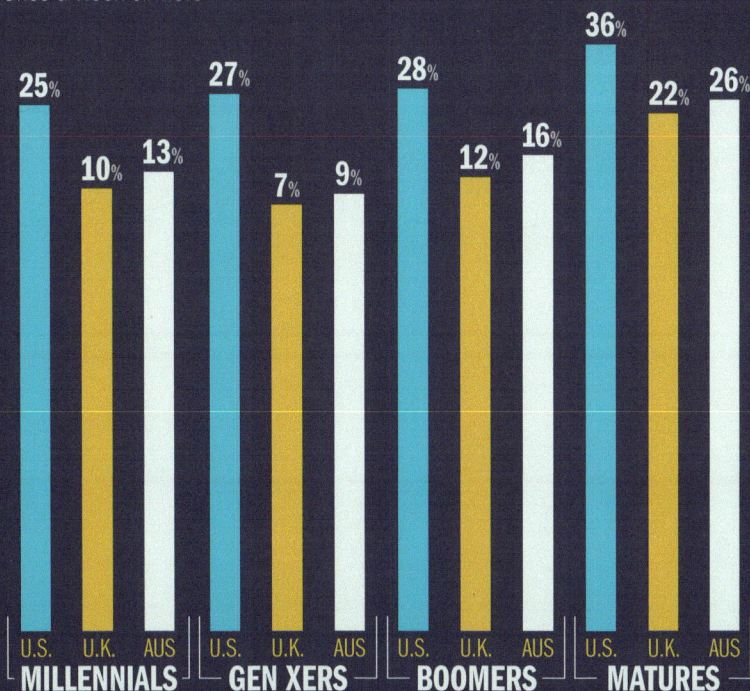

	MILLENNIALS			GEN XERS			BOOMERS			MATURES		
	U.S.	U.K.	AUS	U.S.	U.K.	AUS	U.S.	U.K.	AUS	U.S.	U.K.	AUS
	25%	10%	13%	27%	7%	9%	28%	12%	16%	36%	22%	26%

MILLENNIALS AND RELIGIOUS INVOLVEMENT

Who attends church most?
(at least weekly)

| **25%** | **10%** | **13%** |
| U.S. | U.K. | AUS |

Overwhelmingly, American Millennial donors are much more likely to attend religious services than donors in the U.K. or Australia as only one in ten (10 percent) of U.K. Millennials say they attend religious services weekly, while one in eight Australian Millennials (13 percent) say the same.

Who attends church most?
(at least monthly)

| **49%** | **24%** | **28%** |
| U.S. | U.K. | AUS |

In addition, about twice as many U.S. Millennial donors attend religious services at least monthly compared to their U.K. and Australian counterparts.

Who plans to support a church in the coming year?

U.S.	U.K.	AUS
71%	60%	56%

In keeping with the role of faith and philanthropy, it is of interest that the majority of Millennial donors in each country said they plan to support places of worship in the coming year.

Who plans to give *more* to a church in the coming year?

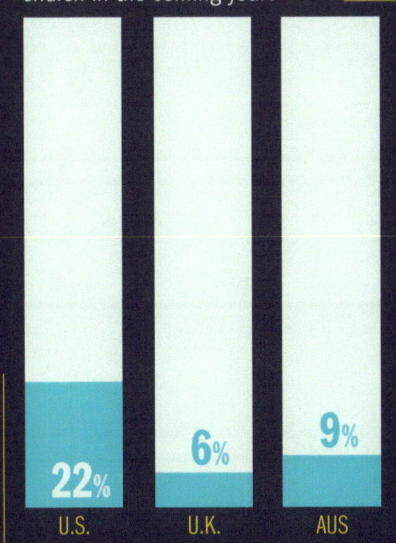

U.S.	U.K.	AUS
22%	6%	9%

Furthermore, 22 percent of U.S. Millennial donors say they plan to give *more* to places of worship in the coming year, whereas only six percent of U.K. Millennials and nine percent of Australian Millennials say the same.

THE ROLE OF TECHNOLOGY

The Millennial generation has grown up with technology as a part of their lives. In fact, the prevalence of technology among Millennials cannot be overstated. The average adult checks their phone 30 times a day, but the average Millennial checks their phone more than 150 times a day.[1]

A Nielsen report released recently showed that adults aged 35 to 49 were found to spend an average of 6 hours, 58 minutes a week on social media networks, compared with 6 hours, 19 minutes for the Millennial group. More predictably, adults 50 and over spent significantly less time on the networks: an average of 4 hours, 9 minutes a week.[2]

Relative to communication, Americans text twice as much as they call, on average.[3] However, roughly 50 percent of adults aged 18 to 24 say text conversations are just as meaningful as a phone call.[4] This same group sends and receives over 128 texts every day.[5]

But important to note is the role of Snapchat in communication, often functioning more as a communication tool than a social media tool. According to a Nielsen study commissioned by the company Snapchat, "Snapchat reaches 41 percent of all 18- to 34-year-olds in the U.S. daily" (roughly 80 million total).[6] "Snapchat now shares 400 million snaps each day, according to CEO Evan Spiegel."[7]

With this information as a backdrop, we wanted to learn how the use of technology by Millennials impacts their giving behavior. What we discovered has direct implications for you and your charity, as your website plays a vital role with Millennials.

[1] https://socialmediaweek.org/newyork/2016/05/31/millennials-check-phones-157-times-per-day/
[2] http://www.nielsen.com/content/dam/corporate/us/en/reports-downloads/2017-reports/2016-nielsen-social-media-report.pdf
[3] http://www.nielsen.com/us/en/insights.html
[4] http://www.experian.com/marketing-services/2013-digital-marketer-report.html?WT.srch=PR_EMS_DMReport_020813_DMReport
[5] https://www.textrequest.com/blog/many-texts-people-send-per-day/
[6] https://www.wsj.com/articles/snapchat-how-brands-reach-millennials-1466568063
[7] https://techcrunch.com/2013/11/19/snapchat-reportedly-sees-more-daily-photos-than-facebook/

First, you better make sure it is easy for a Millennial to give through your website or you stand to lose.

Millennials who have given a gift through a charity's website

51%	49%	33%
U.S.	U.K.	AUS

Of Millennials who have yet to give online, the percentage who say they plan to do so in the future

69%	64%	50%
U.S.	U.K.	AUS

Just over half of Millennials in the U.S. (51 percent) have given a gift through a charity's website. Comparatively, about half (49 percent) of U.K. Millennials and just a third of Australian Millennials (33 percent) have done so.

Of those Millennials who have yet to give online, a significant percentage say they expect to do so at some future time.

Second, when asked what prompted their gift to the charity's website, the plurality of Millennial donors said it was someone asking them via social media. (Note that it was someone asking via social media and *not* the organization making the ask.)

MILLENNIAL DONORS
What percentage are impacted by social media to give online?

37%	39%	33%
U.S.	U.K.	AUS

Additionally, as stated in the 2013 Millennial Impact Report, 45 percent of Millennials were not afraid to ask family and friends for money when they felt strongly about a cause.[1]

Charities are missing a huge opportunity if they aren't tapping into the desire of Millennials to share a worthy cause with their friends and family.

Millennial donors were also more likely than other generations to say that something they saw on the charity website motivated a gift. More than one out of three U.S. Millennials (36 percent) were motivated to give by a charity's website, where only 27 percent of Gen Xers, 14 percent of Boomers and 11 percent of Matures said the same.

In every country surveyed, Millennials were more likely to be motivated by something they saw on a charity's website compared to other generations.

[1] http://www.themillennialimpact.com/research/

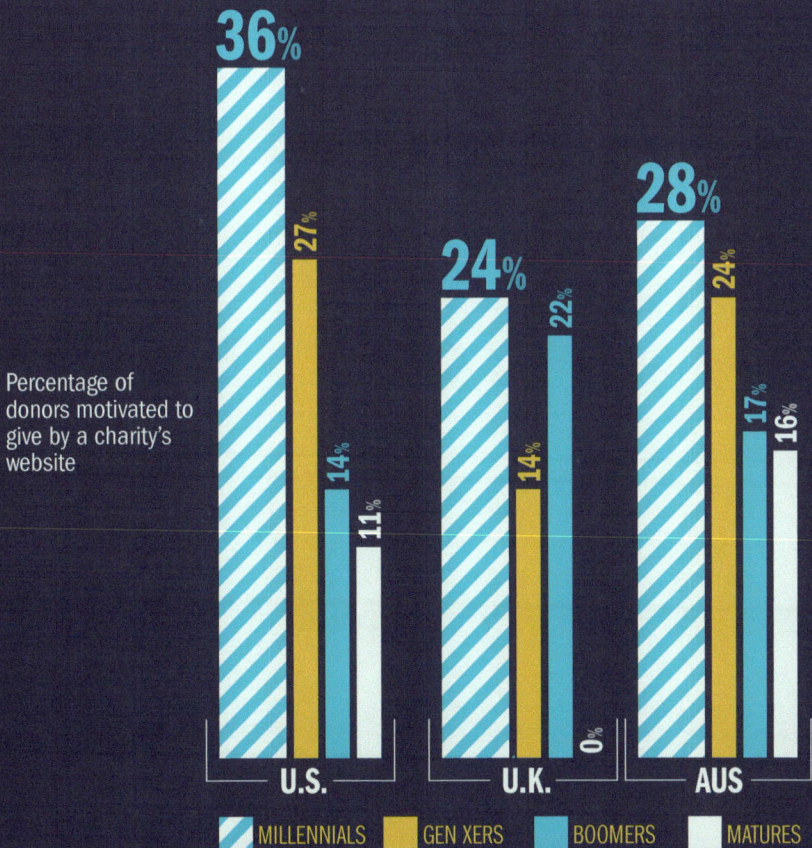

Percentage of donors motivated to give by a charity's website

U.S. — Millennials 36%, Gen Xers 27%, Boomers 14%, Matures 11%

U.K. — Millennials 24%, Gen Xers 14%, Boomers 22%, Matures 0%

AUS — Millennials 28%, Gen Xers 24%, Boomers 17%, Matures 16%

MILLENNIALS   GEN XERS   BOOMERS   MATURES

When it comes to direct mail motivating an online gift, we found that it is still an effective medium for motivating such a response. When asked, about one out of ten Millennials say that they gave to a charity website in response to a direct mail appeal. Not surprisingly, the older the generation the more likely direct mail would motivate an online gift.

MILLENNIALS	10%
GEN XERS	10%
BOOMERS	24%
MATURES	28%

MILLENNIAL DONORS
Who's most likely to give online as a result of direct mail?

U.S.	U.K.	AUS
51%	55%	49%

Interestingly, about one out of ten Millennials in each country surveyed indicated that they had given to a charity's website because of a direct mail appeal.

U.S.	10%
U.K.	11%
AUS	11%

When asked how they prefer to respond to a direct mail appeal, about half of Millennial donors said they preferred to respond using the charity's website, which is much higher than other generations.

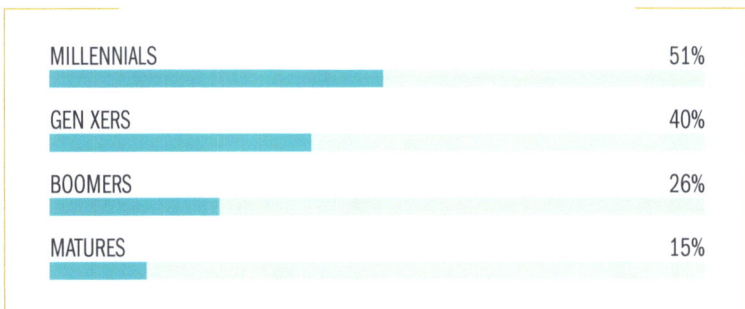

MILLENNIALS	51%
GEN XERS	40%
BOOMERS	26%
MATURES	15%

Not surprisingly, Millennial donors are highly connected to technology, with 99 percent saying they have either a smartphone or tablet. When asked about the use of just a smartphone, it breaks down as follows:

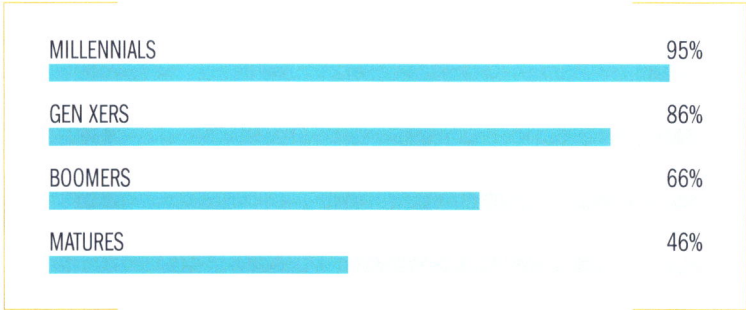

MILLENNIALS	95%
GEN XERS	86%
BOOMERS	66%
MATURES	46%

The 2013 Millennial Impact study indicated that 83 percent of Millennials owned a smartphone at that time.[1] With 95 percent reporting that they own one now, just three years later, it's clear that the prominence of mobile makes it absolutely critical to reach them.

What's really important is that one out of four donors (25 percent) say that they have used their smartphone to give through a charity's website. And even more importantly, 37 percent of Millennial donors say they have done so (which is the same percentage in the U.K. and Australia). We believe it is no longer enough to have your website and giving form mobile optimized, but rather it is imperative to design first for mobile.

---

[1] http://www.themillennialimpact.com/research/

MILLENNIAL DONORS
What percentage have used their smartphone or tablet to give online?

37%	37%	37%
U.S.	U.K.	AUS

OTHER FINDINGS

DO MILLENNIALS FEEL THAT CHARITIES HAVE A WORTHWHILE PLACE IN SOCIETY?

Many have mulled over the notion of the changing role of charities in society around the globe, some even calling into question whether government might be better suited to take over the tasks nonprofits accomplish today.

Indisputably, in the U.K. and the U.S., donors believe that charities are more effective than government in providing important services. In particular, Millennial donors are likely to agree with this sentiment (mean score out of 5).

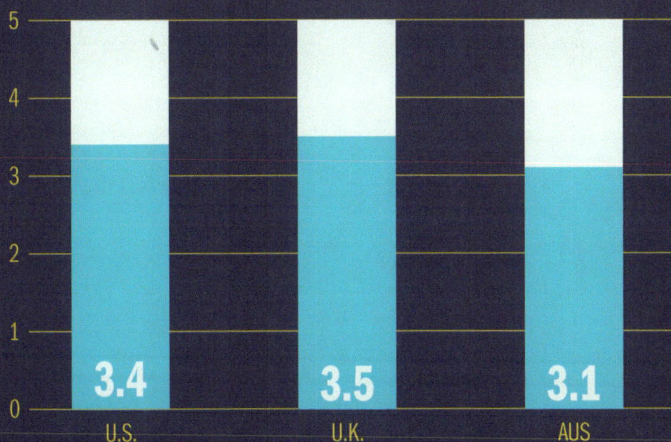

3.4	**3.5**	**3.1**
U.S.	U.K.	AUS

Interestingly, even though donors in Australia support charities to a greater degree than their counterparts in the U.K., they are less likely than their mates to agree that charities are more effective than government.

IS DIRECT MAIL A DEAD COMMUNICATION CHANNEL WITH MILLENNIALS?

Millennial donors in the U.S. say an appeal letter is still likely to motivate a response, while those in the U.K. and Australia are noncommittal (mean score out of 5):

MILLENNIAL DONORS
Who responds most to direct mail?
(mean score out of 5)

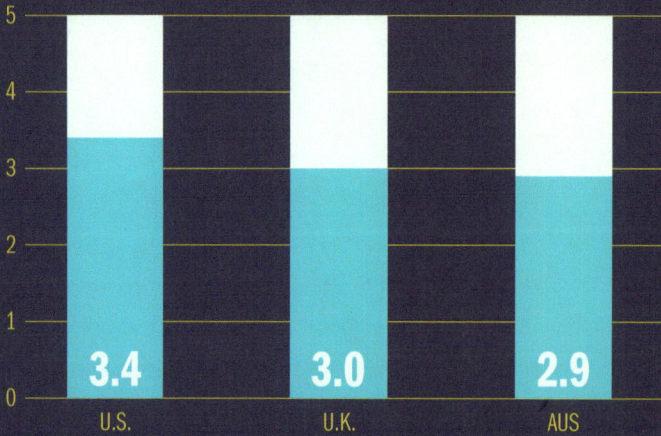

	U.S.	U.K.	AUS
Score	3.4	3.0	2.9

MAIL IS CONSISTENT

According to our study, direct mail is a consistent medium to generate a response in every generation.
(mean score out of 5)

GENERATION	MAIL	EMAIL
MILLENNIALS	3.4	3.7
GEN XERS	3.5	3.4
BOOMERS	3.4	2.8
MATURES	3.6	2.5

DO MATCHING GRANTS WORK WITH MILLENNIALS?

Creating an incentive to give through a matching grant is attractive to Millennial donors (especially U.S. Millennials) as they say that they are motivated to give if the charity says their gift will be matched or multiplied.

MILLENNIAL DONORS
Do matching grants motivate response?

72%	65%	47%
U.S.	U.K.	AUS

Overall, 57 percent of donors say that a matching grant is likely to motivate a gift, so Millennials are actually more likely to be motivated by a match than the average donor.

HOW MUCH COMMUNICATION IS TOO MUCH FOR MILLENNIALS?

About one in two Millennial donors say they expect communication through postal mail at least once per month from charities they support, and two in three say the same about email.

The overwhelming majority of Millennial donors here in the U.S. (81 percent) believe that a phone call at least once a year from a charity they have supported is appropriate and more than one out of three Millennial donors (38 percent) believe it is appropriate to receive a call at least every month.

MILLENNIAL DONORS
What percentage expect postal mail at least monthly from a charity they support?

51%	45%	49%
U.S.	U.K.	AUS

CONCLUSION

U.S. Millennial donors are indeed surprising in many respects. From their level of involvement in religious services to how they interact with traditional media shows that they are not substantially different than other generations.

Would you have predicted that any Millennial would want mail or a phone call from a charity they support? Or that mail and email would be so close as mediums to generate a donation from a Millennial?

Yet, not surprisingly, you can expect them to be the most likely generation to be influenced by a charity's website and to give through that website, being so tied to technology. In addition, with smartphones being so ubiquitous among Millennials, every charity website better be designed for mobile. If not, you stand to lose their engagement.

Finally, U.S. Millennial donors are bullish on the effectiveness of charities to deliver important services compared to the government.

Overall, we believe the data points to one important thing: there is reason for optimism for the future of philanthropy as Millennials mature.

ABOUT DUNHAM+COMPANY

Most nonprofits have a vision to change the world. To right the wrongs, replace injustice with justice, and bring hope where there is none. But their resources restrict the impact they envision.

At Dunham+Company, we understand the struggle to successfully raise more money and reach more donors to impact more lives. Beyond the competition for the charitable dollar, most organizations lack the full complement of skills needed to achieve fundraising success.

That's where we come in.

With nearly 40 years' experience in fundraising and marketing, Dunham+Company knows a thing or two about delivering more results to our clients. It's why we've created our carefully honed 5-step Cause+Effect approach:

- A biblical foundation to fundraising
- Holistic thinking that builds sustainable growth in income
- Integration that connects on multiple levels through multiple channels
- Trusted advisor partnerships that bring the highest level of expertise
- Proprietary data and research tools

Just like the law of cause and effect, we join forces with our client's cause to create a catalytic effect that not only transforms their organization, but touches more lives all around the world.

www.ingramcontent.com/pod-product-compliance
Lightning Source LLC
Chambersburg PA
CBHW041314210326
41599CB00008B/272